MAQALAT

MisrDigital Publications

ISBN: 9781521228081
ASIN: B0727XDV17

First Edition

Wael Abbas

MAQALAT

A Collection of Articles

2006 - 2013

MisrDigital Publications

Index

Article	Page

Introduction

Here are some articles I wrote between the year of 2006 and 2013, some of which are professional op-eds I wrote for some prestigious international media outlets such as The Washington Post, Slate Magazine, BBC and The German News Agency (dpa), while others range from news reports to rants and blog posts.

I decided to collect them all or all what I managed to collect in one place because they are starting to disappear from the Internet and elsewhere, they shed light on an era that has become history now, the era of Mubarak, life and freedoms under his rule.

These articles were written originally by me in English, not in Arabic first and then translated, they tackle in my opinion different significant issues at the time they were written respectively, or just reflect on my personal opinion and personal life at a certain point of that period.

I hope that you find the stories and memories embedded in the articles amusing, I believe even those avid readers of my writings will find many new stories they did not read about from me before.

Now I leave you with the op-ed I wrote for the Washington Post asking the American administration to stop supporting Mubarak, the article about the assassination of late president Anwar Sadat that cost me my job, my testimony about the infamous mass sexual harassment that took place in down town Cairo in the feast of 2006, why I withdrew from the DW's BoBs awards competetion, why I refused to meet president G. W. Bush and many other hopefully interesting stories.

Wael Abbas

Help Our Fight for Real Democracy

The Washington Post, Sunday, May 27, 2007

Last Thursday, I returned to my country, Egypt, after several weeks in the United States on a Freedom House fellowship. I came home full of anxiety. I feared that the authorities would arrest me as soon as I set foot on Egyptian soil.

That didn't happen. But as I went through the airport arrival procedures, I felt that I was being closely watched and followed. Men using walkie-talkies observed me from a distance. When I joined my family members outside the terminal, they, too, told me that they had been watched while waiting for me.

I could still be arrested. And if I am, it will be because I dared to speak the truth about President Hosni Mubarak's regime, which continues to receive billions in foreign aid from the U.S. government -- including funds ostensibly intended to support democracy. It will be because I dared to expose the actions that have made Mubarak's administration one of the world's foremost violators of human rights, according to human rights organizations including Amnesty International, Human Rights Watch and Freedom House.

I am an Egyptian blogger. And the Mubarak regime is out to get me and others like me.

It is engaged in an all-out campaign against those of us who use the Internet to report the truth about what is happening in Egypt. It is spreading rumors about us and targeting us for character assassination. Judges allied with the government have filed lawsuits against more than 50 bloggers, accusing them of blackmail and of defaming Egypt and demanding that their blogs be shut down. Meanwhile, security officials appear on television to claim that the bloggers are violating media and communications laws.

Is this the kind of regime you want your tax money to support?

My story begins in late 2004, several months before the election in which Mubarak was already the preordained winner. People, however, were fed up. After 25 years under this regime, Egyptians had lost all hope of prosperity and of ever being offered economic solutions.

New political movements, such as Kifaya (which means "enough" and is the moniker for the Egyptian Movement for Change), began to call for reform. They held street demonstrations, chanting anti-Mubarak slogans. But no journalists dared cover the protests because of the thousands of security officials who surrounded the activists. So the Egyptian people knew nothing about what was going on.

That's when we bloggers decided to take matters into our own hands. We believed in the people's right to know. I took photos and video footage of the demonstrations and posted them on the Internet, restricting my comments to simple explanations of what was in the pictures. You can write a book and it can all be lies, but one picture can tell the whole story truthfully.

Almost all the opposition and independent newspapers used my photos. I was annoyed at first when some of them stole the material from my blog without crediting me, but in the end I came to feel that it was all right, as long as the message reached the people.

I had about 30,000 visits to my Web site each month. But in May 2005, the situation changed dramatically. On the day of the presidential election, Kifaya, the socialists, the liberals and some Islamists took to the streets to call for a boycott. This time, Mubarak used a new technique. His political party, the National Democratic Party, paid thugs and criminals 20 Egyptian pounds per person (a little over $3) to demonstrate in support of him. The thugs attacked the peaceful demonstrators, tore and burned their banners, sexually harassed female (and some male) activists and journalists. They tore the clothes off one female journalist. I saw men pulling the jeans off a young man and beating him on the buttocks.

I was able to take pictures of what was going on; I was even able to interview one of the thugs, who confessed that he had been paid and that he and others had been brought by bus from the slums specifically to disrupt the peaceful demonstrations. I published the photos and the interview on my blog, and my site received half a million hits in two days. It caused a huge scandal for the government. Newspapers wrote about it for months.

The funny thing is that I got arrested that day, and the police confiscated my camera. But they let me go and gave the camera back after I fooled them into believing that they had deleted all the pictures by removing the batteries. In 2005, digital cameras were still a novelty for police who were accustomed to destroying analog film.

The presidential and parliamentary elections were marred by violence and death. Yes, death -- during the parliamentary elections, nine people were killed by police. It was all documented on my blog. And it was U.S. taxpayer money that funded the new police trucks, clubs, helmets and boots with which the police were equipped.

Of course Mubarak and his party won. But despite all the rigging, Ayman Nour, the leader of the liberal Al-Ghad, or Tomorrow Party, managed to get 1 million votes in the presidential election. And the banned Muslim Brotherhood movement won a fifth of the seats in parliament.

I suppose that could be considered progress. But then what did Mubarak do? He sent Nour to jail on charges of having forged the signatures he collected to establish his party. And today, hundreds of members of the Muslim Brotherhood, as well as some of the movement's parliamentary members, are in prison on charges of having formed an armed movement.

I disagree with the Muslim Brotherhood and its manipulation of Egyptians' religiosity to achieve its political goals. But if we want a democratic country, we can't exclude any political sect.

The world may be afraid of an Islamist movement coming to power in Egypt, and that's why I believe in working on two levels -- advocating democracy while enlightening the people so that they make the right choice when the time comes for real democratic elections. That's why I called my blog Egyptian Awareness. The solution can never lie in supporting and funding a dictatorial regime to suppress the opposition.

Who's left? The bloggers. Those young fellows who think they're hotshot reporters, who dared to practice the first form of citizen journalism in Egypt. The ones who have been such a pain in the neck for the government, exposing corruption, negligence, violations of human rights and freedoms.

In the spring of 2006 -- the spring of democracy, as some have called it -- some judges became fed up with government interference in their rulings and decided to hold a sit-in. In support, a number of bloggers and activists decided to hold a parallel sit-in outside the building where the judges sat. Everyone who took part was arrested. Some of the judges were also assaulted during the raid. All those who were detained were treated inhumanely; some said they were tortured and sodomized.

Eventually, though, the authorities had to release them. And then they had to come up with another way to silence the blogs. They arrested secular blogger Kareem Amer and sentenced him to four years in prison on charges of insulting the president and insulting Islam with statements in his blog. Later, they arrested the Islamist blogger Abdul Monem Mahmoud on charges of belonging to a banned movement, the Muslim Brotherhood. He is now facing trial. Neither secularists nor Islamists are free to express their opinions online under Mubarak's "democratic" regime.

How much is enough to make Americans question why their money goes to support this government? We Egyptians want a fair struggle for our freedom. We'll never have it as long as Mubarak and his corrupt regime are propped up by U.S. aid. All we ask is: Give us a fighting chance.

Help Our Fight for Real Democracy

Big Brothers

In Egypt, Blogging Can Get You Arrested—or Worse.

Slate Magazine, May14, 2007

So, you woke up this morning on the right side of the bed, and you decided to start a blog. Who cares? It is your own choice, you are free to blog as well as not to blog—it depends only on your interests and willingness to express yourself.

Except, in Egypt, the slogan of the State Security Police is: "We care." And they mean it, and not in a good sense.

And so whether to blog is a life-changing decision for Egyptian youth. Of course, you are safe if you decide to write about trivial matters like your day at university or your cat having the hiccups. But once you decide to go political, the police are all ears. Literally. They will tap your phones, harass you with phone calls or by summoning you to their headquarters or stopping you on the street or intruding on your family, even by putting you under arrest.

The Egyptian press is totally under the control of the government. Not only the official newspapers, but also the opposition and independent newspapers, because they are subject to censorship. Bloggers, by contrast, have succeeded in providing neutral and many-sided coverage of events of national import, including the presidential referendum and parliamentary elections; the activities of new movements calling for change in the country; and police brutality toward voters, activists, and ordinary citizens. For example, in connection with the latest election last month, involving President Hosni Mubarak's effort to amend the constitution to make permanent the infamous "law of emergency," bloggers were a repository of reports, photos, and videos showing vote rigging. On my blog, I posted videos of the voting officials themselves checking the "yes" box on people's ballots. I have also posted videos, received from anonymous sources, depicting torture of suspects in police stations—including a sodomizing incident that inflamed public opinion and especially angered the police.

Our readers see blogs as transparent and credible. Not surprisingly, Egypt's less-than-open regime sees them as a threat. The government started losing its patience in the spring of 2006, when a number of bloggers were detained for taking pictures of a sit-in protest, in which they also participated. Bloggers Alaa Seif and Malek Moustapha, and dozens of other activists, including other bloggers, were kept in inhumane conditions, in the company of real criminals, who harassed them under dircct orders from state security. It took 45 days for them to be released. At that point, they were warned against participating in any forthcoming demonstrations.

But some of the bloggers did not listen. They participated in another demonstration to protest other detentions and to support the independence of the judiciary. The police were able to arrest only two of the group but made sure to make an example of them. Kareem El Shaer was beaten severely. Mohammad Sharkawy was taken to a police station, sodomized and tortured, then sent to jail for a few more weeks.

Later, in a separate case, Kareem Amer, who blogged from February 2004 to October 2006, was sentenced to four years in prison—three for insulting Islam and one for insulting the Egyptian president. He had been critical of the country's religious institutions and of the Islamists who are behind attacks on churches. He also had declared himself a secularist. The government singled him out in order to create a precedent, scare other bloggers, and foster an image of bloggers as secular religion-haters. A different sort of function is served by the prosecution of an Islamist blogger, Abdul-Monem Mahmoud, who is facing trial for belonging to the banned Muslim Brotherhood movement. The government went after Mahmoud as part of a campaign against the Brotherhood and to stifle accusations that the police are systematically torturing activists and also ordinary citizens. While Mahmoud was not one of the bloggers who posted videos of torture inside police stations, he was one of the torture victims, and he talked to the media about it.

There is also the case of a documentary filmmaker, Howayda Taha, who has included in her work videos of torture supplied by bloggers—and was then arrested for reconstructing scenes of police torture on her own. The police claimed Taha's torture scenes were faked and were intended to damage Egypt's reputation, though they had given her permission to shoot them. In other words, they set her up. And the effect, of course, is to silence anyone who has new videos and wants to participate in the campaign against torture. Several policemen are on trial on torture-related charges as a result of the videos that the bloggers have published. One has already been sentenced to a year in prison. The government is desperate to put an end to this embarrassment.

The government is also forcing lesser-known young bloggers to shut down their blogs. One incident involved a Christian woman from Upper Egypt who criticized the government's treatment of Christians. The police detained her for a while and forced her to shut down her blog. The police also shut down the blog of a woman in her early 20s who criticized the policies of Libya. These detentions show how the government uses fear to stymie bloggers whose arrests go relatively unnoticed.

Sometimes, I wish that I were among the bloggers who have been arrested. What can make a person in his right senses wish to go to jail? The alternative techniques that Egyptian security used on me. When I managed to evade arrest several times, the police started making threatening phone calls, saying that if I did not cooperate, they would arrest me. You're a good guy, they told me. You are new. Your name came up in the investigations, but we don't want to arrest you. If you cooperate, we will be like your older brothers. If you don't, it will create scandal for your family. They gave me a phone number so I could think over their offer and use it when I was ready to talk. Instead, I published the conversations on my blog. They never called me again.

But when I continued blogging, gaining attention and stirring public opinion in Egypt and internationally, the government tried another technique: character assassination. The assistant of the Egyptian interior minister for legal affairs appeared on television to say that I had a criminal record. He did this three times on different stations and different talk shows; luckily, I have videos of that, as well, here and here. I had to respond by publishing my criminal record on my blog. It has a stamp saying "no criminal charges."

Meanwhile, journalists at official newspapers have continued to tarnish my reputation. Their latest tactic is to spread rumors via the Internet that are calculated to diminish my credibility. They say that I converted to Christianity or that I'm a homosexual, neither of which can be tolerated in the Egyptian culture (and neither of which are true).

Now I'm getting information that the government's next step will be to send me to jail on charges of espionage and homosexuality. I'm told they will use the fact that I'm spending this month in the United States as part of a Freedom House fellowship program—and as an intern at *Slate*—to back up those charges.

So, what would you prefer? To go to jail with honor as a political dissident? Or to have your reputation tarnished with charges like these? The bloggers in Egypt are the last independent voice. If we are silenced, no protests will be heard in Egypt, not only now, but for the coming quarter- or even half-century. And so the choice to blog is not only serious, but necessary.

Blogging in the Middle East
A tough choice
DPA, Thursday September 14, 2006

Creating a blog in a Western country is a very private decision, depending only on one's interests and a willingness to express oneself. Such is not the case in the Middle East, where becoming a blogger can be a life-changing decision attracting phone taps, official harassment or even arrest.

For Egypt's less-than-open regime, bloggers have been a veritable "pain in the neck," covering presidential and parliamentary elections as well as the activities of all the new movements calling for change in the country.

The bloggers have been winning favour with audiences who see them as transparent and credible as they provide reports and photos that expose vote rigging, corruption and police brutality. By using unorthodox methods and avoiding censorship, bloggers have excelled over conventional media.

But one Egyptian blogger, Alaa Seif owner of Manalaa.net, paid the price.

In a major indication that the Egyptian government has lost its patience with bloggers, Seif recently spent 45 days in detention for taking pictures of a sit-in protest.

While some Egyptian bloggers choose to disclose their identities and expose themselves to the authorities, bloggers in other of the region's countries do not have that option.

The Iranian blogger revolution for example was started in Canada by Iranian emigre Hussein Derakhshan, nicknamed Hoder. His blog was followed by huge numbers of others written anonymously in Iran. As a result of this revolution, government officials - including President Mahmud Ahmadinajad - have their own blogs.

In 2003, Iran became the first country in the world to jail a blogger, journalist Sina Matlabi, who was jailed for endangering the security of the state. Iran was also first in issuing laws regulating activity on the Internet.

In 2005 the owner of Bahrainonline.com Ali Abdulemam was arrested in Bahrain on accusations of violating press law, inciting hatred and threatening to destabilize the country.

Sami Bin-Gharbiya, the Tunisian owner of Kitab.nl, is destined to become a refugee both physically and virtually. He lives in Holland as a political refugee and he is banned from the Tunisian blog aggregator (a software that displays news feeds on blogs) so he took refuge in the Egyptian blog aggregator hosted by Manalaa.net.

A country where blogging is becoming popular is Morocco. Following in the footsteps of their Egyptian counterparts, Morocco's small community of bloggers are making their voices heard. For example, a report published on Jankari.org about how government money was being spent on official trips abroad lead to the sacking of a high government official.

In Lebanon where the press is relatively free bloggers have taken a different approach, using their blogs to raise funds for the victims of the 33-day war between Israel and Hizbullah. One example was the Lebanese Blogger Forum, which also posted photos, cartoons and video coverage of the war.

To the south, Israelis used their blogs to justify their country's war in Lebanon. "Please understand us, our government has a duty to protect civilians from Hizbullah's rocket attacks," says Israellycool.

Even in Saudi Arabia, where blogging lies under a stifling theocratic shroud, bloggers succeeded in lobbying against censorship. In August when the famous blog Saudijeans.org was blocked, a group of Saudis organized a strike in which they stopped blogging for 27 days. This succeeded in convincing the authorities to remove the block.

This is the interview that cost me my job as the middle east correspondent of Deutsche Presse Agentur (dpa) and landed late PM Talaat Sadat a sentence in a military jail.

Anwar Sadat still revered in Egypt

DPA, Tuesday October 3, 2006

Former Egyptian president Anwar Sadat was watching an aerial display of Mirages at a military parade on October 6, 1981, the eighth anniversary of the Yom Kippur war with Israel, when two hand grenades exploded, gunmen jumped off a military truck and opened fire on the presidential podium. Although there were supposed to have been four rings of security around the president, witnesses said nothing was done to stop the attackers.

They fired shots for slightly over a minute killing Sadat, revered by most Egyptians as the hero of war and peace.

Now that Egypt prepares to celebrate the 25th anniversary of the assassination, doubt is still cast on the incident.

The precision with which the attack was executed raised suspicions that it could not possibly have been done without the use of high level intelligence information and inside help.

"What happened on the October 6, 1981 was a limited military coup conducted by the vice president Hosny Mubarak, the Minister of Defence Colonel Abu Ghazala and their co-conspirators," says opposition MP Talaat Sadat who is also the nephew of late president Anwar Sadat.

Talaat Sadat says: "They started hammering nails in the coffin of Sadat by killing Ahmad Badawy, the minister of defence, and the 14 heads of the Egyptian army branches in a highly controversial and questionable helicopter crash in March 1981 replacing them with officers loyal to Mubarak that will help with the coup. The head of the republican guard was also changed and so was the head of the intelligence agency".

"My uncle intended to sack Mubarak replacing him with Mustapha Khaleel. This intention was recorded in a television interview with the late broadcaster Hemmat Moustapha, but it was never aired of course", said MP Sadat.

Talaat believes that Mubarak did not order a real investigation into the assassination because he stood behind it.

An independent investigation was initiated by human rights activist Saaduldeen Ibraheem in 1999, but it stopped suddenly because Ibraheem was accused of spying for the United States and was imprisoned.

"There were many who would benefit from the death of Sadat especially that he was not in good terms with the then new American administration under Regan," said Talaat.

The Egyptian ambassador in Washington, then Ashraf Ghourbal, sent a telegram to Sadat when Mubarak was visiting the United states before the assassination. He complained that he had not attended Mubarak's meeting with the CIA, unlike all the other meetings during the visit, Talaat Sadat added.

Talaat claims that both the US and Israel benefited from Anwar Sadat's death.

"Sadat angered the United States when he exposed the role Egypt played in the war in Afghanistan to help the US in response to the American refusal to sell AWAX planes to Saudi Arabia though Egyptian political relations with Saudi was cut at the time."

"Sadat also succeeded through intelligence info to expose an Israeli attempt to invade Lebanon in 1981 callcd operation Galilee. He also exposed the role Israel played in the seizure of the American embassy in Tehran in 1979. And finally Israel wanted to stop its upcoming withdrawal from Sinai in April 25, 1982 to a standstill".

The Soviet Union also benefited from Sadat's death, according to Talaat Sadat. His uncle had managed to rid Egypt of Soviet influence imposed during former president Gamal Abdul Nasser's tenure thus prompted the Soviet

Union to stir up opposition to Sadat resulting in the controversial September 1981 mass arrests.

Talaat Sadat also claims that the Arab countries, or the so-called rejection front, to the peace treaty between Egypt and Israel benefited from his death. If Sadat had succeeded in solving the Palestinian issue, this would have exposed all the Arab leaders involved.

He adds: "Though Iraq headed the rejection front, Sadat gave Saddam weapons during the war with Iran. But because of his democratic reforms when he gave independence to the justice, freedom to labour unions, political parties and the press, some Arab and African countries were afraid that democracy in Egypt will infect them. May God rest his Soul; he was the hero of war and peace".

Minister Faces Fire over Islamic Veil Controversy

DPA Published: Tuesday November 28, 2006

The Egyptian Minister of Culture has been left alone to face a storm of criticism over his views on the Islamic veil after most government officials have sided with his critics or refused to back him up.

Farouk Hosni the Egyptian Minister of Culture sparked the controversy when he described the growing popularity of the Islamic veil in Egypt as "a regressive trend," in an interview with an Egyptian newspaper.

In the Egyptian parliament Monday, 130 members demanded the resignation of the minister. The campaign against him united the Muslim Brotherhood, Egypt's main opposition movement which controls one fifth of the seats in parliament, and the ruling National Democratic Party (NDP) to which he belongs.

Fifty NDP parliament members signed the petition demanding the minister's resignation.

The trial of Hosni for scorning religion was also demanded by 93 MPs, who said that their wives and daughters wore the Islamic veil.

The minister in an interview published last week with the Egyptian independent daily newspaper al-Masri al-Youm said: "There was an age when our mothers went to university and worked without the veil. It is in that spirit that we grew up, so why this regression?"

Hosni also said: "Each woman with her beautiful hair is like a flower and should not be concealed from the view of others," adding that "religion today focuses on appearances too much."

Some religious scholars are debating whether Hosni can be considered a non-believer or not, something which might incite militant extremists.

For this reason Hosni reportedly asked the ministry of interior to increase security around him.

Observers say that Egypt is becoming an increasingly conservative society although it was considered to be one of the most liberal Arab countries in the 60s and 70s.

Owing to deteriorating economic conditions, a large number of Egyptians were forced to work in the oil-rich Arab countries of the Gulf. They absorbed their culture and brought it back to Egypt.

"They all distance themselves away when a subject like that is brought up", said Iqbal Baraka, author of the controversial book, The Veil.

Nobody "wants to be pulled inside the storm," added Baraka, who is also the editor in chief of Hawa (Eve) magazine, which has praised the courage of the minister.

Her book was published in 2002, but it was not until 2006 that it caused controversy when the Mufti attacked it and other religious scholars demanded it to be banned.

In her book, Baraka uses research methods to prove that the veil is not Islamic, nor does its use originate in the Koran.

Her book argues that it is merely a traditional costume introduced to cope with the lifestyle in the desert to protect both men and women from the sun and the sandstorms. She says it started 2,000 years before Islam in Assyria.

"Young people are unfortunately ignorant," comments Barakat. "Their knowledge about Islam is limited, and they received their information from Saudi financed religious satellite channels."

Hosni did not attend the parliamentary session. However, he sent a paper to be read by the head of the parliament, in which he said: "It was only my personal opinion, and not a press statement.

My words were taken out of context from a conversation that was off the record. The opinion about the veil is only for the religious scholars to decide. I did not mean what some tried to make it look like, I respect Egyptian veiled women."

The controversy however has not abated and the minister will now have to answer questions before two parliamentary committees, the religious affairs committee and the cultural affairs committee.

Intellectuals in Egypt, including leftist and liberal opposition, have come out in favour of the minister.

They consider what has happened to be a form of intellectual terrorism and a campaign against freedom of speech.

This is the first time that an Egyptian minister has come under heavy criticism from his own side. It is unprecedented as even when a minister is accused of corruption or negligence the party protects him.

Farouk Hosni has been in office for 19 years. Last year, his resignation was refused after accusations of negligence when dozens were killed in a state-owned theatre in Upper Egypt.

Protests were held in Egyptian universities against the minister's remarks, and more protests are planned in the coming few days.

Egyptian state-owned television channels do not allow women wearing the Islamic veil to present programmes.

Televised Fatwas Spark Debate Among Islamic Scholars

DPA, Wednesday October 18, 2006

Talk shows in Oprah Winfrey style are the latest to hit Arab broadcasters and they are accompanied by mounting debate on the value of their contents and their effect on values in conservative Arab societies. Unlike talk shows in the west which focus mainly on social and political issues, some Arab talk shows add religion to the mix, and this involves hosting religious scholars. The audience deem their opinions to be Fatwas or religious decrees which prompt heated debate on the eligibility to issue them.

The legitimacy of suicide attacks was one of the issues on which opinions among religious scholars diverged. Some considered it a courageous form of resisting a mighty enemy while others considered it merely illegitimate suicide.

This debate was renewed recently when a sheikh from al-Azhar confirmed on a talk show a controversial Hadith, a saying or practice by Prophet Mohammad collected after his death.

According to the Hadith, women were advised to breast-feed their male servants or office colleagues so that they assume the status of her sons. This would prohibit sexual intercourse between them and the woman in turn would

31

become immune from seduction and harassment by them, the sheikh claimed.

Observers in Cairo note, however, that there have been no recent reports about women actually performing such practices in the Arab world.

But other sheikhs consider this particular Hadith false, while the majority simply avoids discussing it. It is considered very grave to claim that a Hadith attributed to Prophet Mohammad is false, and for this reason many Muslim scholars avoid the matter altogether.

Dr Abdul Moneim Abul Fotouh, a member of the Guidance office of the Muslim Brotherhood movement says: "We don't have a church or a pope and we have a variety of schools of Islamic Fiqh (the science of Islamic jurisprudence). In my opinion, this is healthy and I'm proud of it, but Islam is organized, and anybody who seeks guidance or Fatwa should go directly to religious institutions such as al-Azhar."

"As a doctor must be a holder of a degree in medicine, a Mufti must be a holder of a degree in religion," he added.

The Islamic thinker, Dr Moustafa al-Shak'a, a member of the Islamic Research Centre, believes a Mufti must be qualified to issue Fatwas and must study the Koran, Hadith, the biography of Prophet Mohammad and Islamic history.

"Those Muftis of satellite channels are mostly not qualified though some of them might have a PhD, they tend to use body language in order to fool people, they might have some influence and some of them have big names but surely they should have never practiced Iftaa (the act of issuing a fatwa).

"Those who are resisting an enemy have other alternatives for suicide operations, suicide is forbidden in Islam," said Dr Shak'a.

Dr Shak'a recommends that if somebody is looking for a Fatwa, he should seek it in the right place, but not on television. The Mufti of Egypt and his assistants can help and a telephone number has been assigned for Fatwas. The Islamic Research Centre and the Fatwa division of al-Azhar can also provide information.

I Withdraw From The BOBs Awards

MisrDigital, Tuesday, 23 April 2013

Due to the lack of fairness of competition I announce that I withdraw from The BOBs awards competition. As it has become known and proven that some Mauritanian bloggers resorted to using electronic software for voting for the Mauritanian Candidate Nasser Weddady. Nasser is a dear friend of mine and I'm sure he has nothing to do with this but the enthusiasm of some of his followers is what makes this competition unfair. Nasser and me have worked for years against corruption and election rigging in our countries.

The BOBs awards voting have always been marred in corruption and this is not the first time, and the management have failed to solve these corruption and technical issues: I was removed before from the category I was running for in 2005 by an Egyptian Judge and put in a category I did not run for and never intended to! and the following year a Tunisian blogger used a software to increase her votes overnight from second place to first place and was given the award. And obviously the voting system was not repaired since then.

I'm a winner of many prestigious International awards like The Knight Journalism Award 2007 and The Hellman Hammett Award 2008, I was named by CNN Middle East's

Most Influential Person of the year 2007, I was named by the BBC one of the most influential people of the year 2006, I was named by Forbes Magazine, Foreign Policy Magazine and Arabian Business Magazine one of the most influential Arabs in 2011 thank god.

I have boycotted the BOBs for several years and I did not care what they do, and even this year my nomination was a surprise for me and I did not want it! so I announce that I can't take this shit anymore so please remove me and don't consider adding me any more!

Thank you!

In Your Face
Misrdigital, Friday, 01 October 2010

Yes, I'm very well aware I'm not good looking and maybe uncool and unhip to some people each according to their own standards, I have no illusions about it, and I need no enlightenment about it thank you! but mind you! that doesn't mean people should assume I'm insecure about it at all, thus they can tread on me or take me lightly.

But unfortunately people sometimes don't accept that, and out of their naiivity tend to play the insecure card in a face-off with me, sometimes those people include but not limited to: State Security, political opponents, friends who loathe or envy you, girlfriends who want to control you and make you feel inferior to them, etc., which to their surprise backfires on them and their own insecurities.

Yes I know it challenges the norms people are used to when it comes to "ugly poor pathetic sods", but believe it or not it happened that I'm flamboyant and I flaunt it, I'm one die-hard narcissistic son of a bitch who never lacks self-esteem or backs down no matter what, and I have a fine taste in women and I deliberately don't recognize or grace the phrase: "out of your league".

So why exactly should that offend you? do I make you feel little? or maybe threatened and insecure yourself? So fuck your norms and fuck what you believe in, I don't tread lightly, I'm here and on your TV and in your favorite newspaper, I do something I love and believe in and people

36

respect me for that, I feel great about myself and never sorry for it, and I still believe there are people in this world who are objective and secure enough - unlike you - to accept me the way that I am, and that might be the only thing I have illusions about, other than that KOSS OMM EL TENNEEN as a dear friend once said!

I Turned Down an Invitation to Meet up With Bush

MisrDigital, Thursday, 04 December 2008

I received a phone call from a senior employee in the American Embassy yesterday inviting me to meet up with President Bush - yes, he still is the president until Obama's official inauguration ceremony.

To be honest, I was taken by surprise but I remembered that Bush did meet up with an Iraqi blogger. He might be interested in the Iraqi blogger because of the Iraqi invasion but why would he want to meet me? If the interview is related to my being a journalist or a blogger who gets the opportunity to hammer him with questions then cool but meeting Bush in itself is not an honor .. why would I consider meeting him?

Bush is neither my president nor my father; he is not the world's legal guardian as he would like to imagine. Bush is not a symbol of anything honorable to honor anyone who meets him; Meeting Bush would tarnish an honest man's reputation - it is by far nothing worthy of pride.

I owe Bush nothing and he owes me nothing and even if he has something that I might want, I no longer want it. I am inherently against any American involvement in the Egyptian business be it good or bad. I just want him to hold his peace and stop supporting the Egyptian regime.

Put the Iraqi invasion aside with all the other worldwide disasters that Bush brought on the world, it is more than enough for me that Bush calls president Mubarak "a man of peace".

I did not reject the invitation for fear of criticism and live skinning of some political parties in Egypt because I can safely assume that we do not have anything even close to political parties in Egypt.

Simply why would I be interested in meeting a person like Bush - he is not a Nelson Mandela or a Gandhi or a Mother Teresa -may she rest in peace.

Had this been an invitation to meet Obama - no offense - I would have gladly accepted it. At least I would have had the pleasure of meeting the man before he assumes office and dirties his hands.

Now people love him and I would have liked to meet him when people still love him. I would have had the honor of meeting the icon of change in American history. He is the symbol of a truly democratically elected president. This is the model that we would like to see all over the world, starting with Egypt.

I might even have the audacity to say that Obama's victory is a new landmark since the African American civil rights movement and its symbols - namely Martin Luther King and Malcolm X.

But who is this Bush and what does he represent? I serve the causes of political and individual freedom and fighting oppression, violence, and dictatorship so how does Bush serve my cause?

The old American cabinet knows that they are on their way out so they decided to create havoc on their way out. They also decided to honor some activists when in fact by doing so America is disgracing them. They want to take credit for their strife and success before its fifteen minutes of fame are over.

I love Americans as people and every time I visit America, it is because the Americans are supportive of me and my cause.... Maybe America is not the ideal solution for freedom of press and political parties but still it's civil society is an interesting experience to study and analyze.

Asshole!

Misrdigital, Saturday, 14 April 2007

I have a question!

Is it punishable by American laws to insult a federal officer on a blog? Because if it is not I'd like to insult the federal officer who stopped me in JFK airport in New York because the mother fucker did not like my name and because of that I missed my flight to Washington DC.

Obviously the mother fucken police is the same everywhere.

In December 2006 I was chosen by the BBC as one of the most influential people in the world along with Kofi Annan, Desmond Tutu and Wole Soyinka, and was asked to record a new year message to be aired on radio.

My New Year Message on BBC
BBC, Monday, 25 December 2006

My message at the beginning of a new year is not to a person, but rather to a thing. My message is to this marvelous thing called the Internet, The Jinni that goes everywhere to everyone traveling through wires and cables and even through thin air.

This jinni was the one to open the jar called mainstream media that we were kept in for decades. The jinni opened the jar and let us out once and for good, the jinni gave us unlimited freedom of expression - something we had never had.

And the bloggers are the most thankful of all for this bliss, especially those of the third world.

But this jinni frightens some governments, because it made things get out of hand for them -- the time when they thought they had control over everything has come to an end, their control and censorship of the press and the air waves is over. And no matter how hard they try to put it back in the jar, it surprisingly manages to escape.

Dear jinni, we are counting on you, to give our people the real picture, without distortion, without censorship and without hidden agendas, we are counting on you to expose corruption, negligence and violations of human rights. And grant us one more wish for the New Year, free Ayman Nour, free Talaat Sadat and free all the prisoners of conscience in Egypt and all over the world.

A Push in The Right Direction

Knight Award Acceptance Speech
ICFJ Award Dinner, November 13, 2007

Ladies and Gentlemen,

I'd like to thank the International Center for Journalists and the Knight Foundation for this prestigious award, and for their recognition of the bloggers worldwide, and in Egypt in particular.

I believe it is the first time a blogger has received a journalism award. Back in my country, they do not receive awards. Instead, all that bloggers receive are threats, intimidation, accusations of breaking the law – and sometimes jail sentences.

This Award came at a critical time. I had started to question what I was doing, and whether it would change anything in my country for the better. It was natural that I questioned my work because my work changed my life – and unfortunately, it was a change for the worse. I am now classified as an opponent of the government. I lost my job as a journalist and now it is extremely difficult to get a decent job and at the same time continue blogging.

This Award has given me new hope and faith that I am pushing in the right direction. It's a vote of confidence not just in me, but also in the growing community of bloggers in Egypt and the region. I see it as a sign that I must keep going.

I never wanted my name to be associated with violence, torture and police brutality. I never wanted to deal with issues such as corruption, forgery, bribery and sexual harassment. All I wanted was for my country to change, to become more democratic and to recognize the basic rights of its citizens. So, I focused my work on making people aware of what was going on and helping them understand their rights. I feel now that it's an honor to receive an Award that supports and promotes the things that are most important to me.

The fight against a regime that is both cruel and stubborn, a regime that signs international treaties, but seldom recognizes them or puts them into action, will be long and bitter. It's a regime that uses its alliances with world powers as a weapon against its own people. But as long as there are people who stand by the truth and support those who tell the truth, there is hope for change.

Finally, I'd like to thank Knight Fellow Stephen Franklin for nominating me. I also would like to thank my family, who did not know what I was doing behind their backs. When they found out, of course they freaked out at first, but then understood and respected my work.

I would like to dedicate this award to all the Egyptian bloggers who have dared to speak up, demonstrate and protest, and pay the price. They could have gone through life the easy way. Instead, they chose to blog.

Testimony on Mass Sexual Harassment

The Cynthia Nelson Institute, AUC, Monday, December 4, 2006

It was supposed to be the usual feast celebration. Every year the ministry of interior bores us with the usual statement before the feast, whether on television or in the press: "the police will be highly alert in order to enable the Egyptians to enjoy the feast".

I usually don't go out during the feast days, but that very first day of Eid I happened to be on duty. I finished work and headed to down town to chill out with some friends. We were sitting in an outdoor café when a friend came to alert us that hell was breaking loose in the vicinity of Cinema Metro and Cinema Miami.

He started telling us about women being sexually harassed by huge numbers of men. His sentences comprised descriptions like: torn clothes, shattered ticket windows and a surprising absence of the police.

We were astounded. At first we did not quite believe him. We thought it must just be the usual Eid entertainment; guys trying to talk to girls, mild flirting, just hanging out, the normal stuff. We grew curious and went to see the broken ticket windows of Cinema Metro that would make a good picture or two.

Our group was made up of Reuters photographer Abdul Nasser Al Nouri, Al Karama newspaper photographer Peter Alfred, blogger and activist Malek Moustafa, blogger and activist Mohammad Gamal, Mohammad Al Sharkawy and several other bloggers, activists and professional journalists and myself. We were around ten, all of us saw what happened and some of us managed to take pictures.

Arriving at the scene we immediately noticed the destroyed ticket windows of the cinema, but other than that everything seemed normal except for the expected crowds outside the cinema during the feast days.

But all of a sudden dozens of guys started running in a certain direction. We followed. They were after a girl, encircled her and started touching and groping her. The girl ran and stumbled. They tried to stop her, but finally she was able to take refuge inside a restaurant. They surrounded the restaurant. The workers in there came out and tried to drive them away. A policeman tried to use his club but in vain.

Their attention was not diverted from the girl inside until one of them shouted: "another one at Cinema Miami". Only then did they all head in the direction of the other woman. The tragedy was repeated, and kept repeating itself till midnight as I was told by other witnesses the next day.

No matter how a woman was dressed, veiled or unveiled, young or old, alone or accompanied by a father, husband, brother or friend, it all made no difference. To them, anything that smelled like a female and moved was a target.

This unfortunate event took place more than once during the same day, by various groups of men, attacking many girls in different streets in the same vicinity simultaneously. Two girls dressed in the gulfi Abaya were surrounded, separated and harassed. One of them took refuge in the entrance of a building and the janitors protected her. A security guy even drew his gun to drive away the gangs.

Another girl took refuge inside a shop whose owners had to pull down the shutters to protect her. They were so furious at what was happening that they decided to take things into their own hands, using clubs, whips and even broom sticks to rescue the other girls attacked outside the shop.

Even girls inside cars were harassed. A group of men tried to pull a girl out of a taxi. Another girl was withdrawing money from an ATM machine when she found herself surrounded by dozens who started touching and groping her. She was only rescued by a cab driver who took her inside his car, but the men did not like that and surrounded the taxi. Eventually he was able to flee with the girl in his car.

There were, however, several other accounts of girls that were pulled out of taxis, and noble taxi drivers who insisted on saving them ended up with their taxi windows destroyed. Several eyewitnesses said that some of these girls had their clothes torn off and there were numerous other accounts on the internet and in the printed press of even more horrific incidents of sexual harassment, not only in Cairo, but also in Alexandria and Mansoura.

Unlike in peaceful protests where the police forces outnumber the demonstrators, there was less than half a dozen policemen at the scene. They were only keen on protecting the cinemas and the movie stars who attended their premiers.

They saw everything and did nothing despite the fact that the police station was just a few blocks away, so they could've asked for whatever extra forces needed to contain the chaos. The officers had walkie talkies, they could have asked for backup, but still didn't. Their only source of nuisance seemed to be "us" and our taking pictures. We approached them and asked them to act promptly, but they gave the feeble excuse that because of the feast they were outnumbered. They even tried to entice us to stop taking pictures by offering to let us into any of the cinemas to watch the movies for free.

We were speechless and helpless. Of course we could not fight all these numbers of angry men in the midst of such sexual frenzy. I was carrying a backpack with a laptop inside, not prepared at all for a street fight, so we decided to warn women and girls coming down the street, explain to them and ask them to change their route. This seemed to be the only helping hand we could lend on that crazy crazy night.

What was really shocking was that the same scenario repeated itself the following day and the day after on Talaat Harb street as well as several other places down town.

That day I did not have a professional camera. I only had the camera installed in my mobile phone. It was dark, too crowded and naturally people did not react too well to the fact that I was taking pictures. One security guard cocked his gun in my face to make me stop. I didn't blame him. He thought it was scandalous, and indeed it was.

Due to the technical shortage, the pictures did not come out good, hence the reaction of the ministry of interior and some official newspapers that claimed that my photos were fabricated. The Reuters photographer in our group did not think highly of his photos either and he deleted them. As for Peter from Al Karama, and although his pictures were unclear as well he still kept them for the next issue of his weekly newspaper.

I uploaded my pics onto the computer, and decided to keep them for later use. Malek, Jimmy and Sharkawy all published their accounts of the incident in their respective blogs. The responses they received were massive. There was a whole gamut of people's reactions. While some were shocked, others doubted the whole episode. Malek called me and asked me to publish the pictures, and only then that things got messier.

It had never happened to me before that anybody doubted the credibility of my photos, which are often used by most independent and opposition newspapers, and even some official newspapers resort to using them. The poor quality of the mobile phone down town photos seemed to be a good opportunity for some people to attack my credibility.

Reports published in official newspapers showed that there was an intention to fabricate a case against me for spreading rumours. Some journalists voiced suspicions in my report of the incident and attacked me personally. My family started receiving weird phone calls of people trying to locate me. Security officials attacked me severely on television and tried to make people believe that I had a criminal history.

I was only saved by some TV programmes which hosted eyewitnesses who were there during the crisis and who confirmed what I said, but it is such a shame that the ministry of interior would go that far and that low in order to cover up for their negligence.

What Happens Next if Saddam is Convicted?

DPA, Nov 3, 2006

Dujail is a small Shiite town in Iraq. It is located some 65 kilometres north of Iraq's capital, Baghdad, and has around 10,000 inhabitants. But this small town is about to play a big part in the life of Iraq's former dictator Saddam Hussein.

On July 8, 1982 an unsuccessful assassination attempt targeted Saddam while he was visiting the town. His convoy was engaged in a three-hour firefight but the Iraqi dictator escaped unharmed.

Later, at Saddam's orders, a total of 143 males in the town were killed or executed, including a number of 13-year-old boys, in a reprisal for the failed assassination attempt. Approximately 1,500 Shiites were incarcerated and tortured, while others, including women and children, were sent to desert camps. Saddam's regime destroyed the town and then rebuilt it. In addition, 1,000 square kilometers of farmland were destroyed and the regime did not allow any planting for 10 years.

Now, 24 years after the events, Hussein and seven other defendants are being tried for crimes against humanity. The trial, the first of a series against Saddam, began before the Iraqi Special Tribunal on October 19, 2005.
A verdict in the Dujail case is reportedly to be announced on Sunday fifth of November - raising many questions for Iraqis: If Saddam was convicted, what will it mean for Iraq,

how will it affect the political process, will sectarian violence escalate further, and what does it mean in the international context? And - does the timing have anything to do with the US congressional elections?

Members of the defense committee of Saddam and his aides consider the trial to be illegal.

The committee also contends that it is no accident that the verdict is to be announced on November 5 - just two days before the US congressional elections.

Hussein had told the court last July: 'I advise you as an Iraqi, if you were in a circumstance in which you have to issue a death penalty, you have to remember that Saddam is a military man and in this case the verdict should be death by shooting not by hanging.'

If back then supporters of Saddam in his home town Tikrit protested against the trial, the question now is whether the protests will be more widespread if Saddam is convicted. There is no way of predicting, analysts say, pointing out that there are no opinion polls about Saddam since he is no longer the main issue in Iraq.

Iraq is neck deep in sectarian violence between Sunnis and Shiites with no signs in sight that this will end soon. Shiites mainly hate Saddam. And although whenever an insurgent attack happens the Iraqi government divides the blame equally between the so-called Saddamists and the extreme Sunni insurgents, in reality it is the extreme Sunni insurgents who are behind the majority of the attacks. It cannot be said that this latter group are so particularly in love with Saddam that the violence would escalate further if the former leader is convicted.

But being on the safe side, the defense ministry has ordered all Iraqi troops now on leave to return to their barracks in a precautionary measure to be prepared for any possible escalation of insurgent attacks.

About The Author

Wael Abbas

- Knight International Award for Journalistic Excellence 2007
- CNN Middle East Person of the Year 2007
- BBC World Service Most Influential People 2006
- Human Rights Watch's Hellman/Hammett Award 2006
- Honorary Member of the American Bar Association (ABA) since 2007
- Knight International Advisory Committee member since 2007
- Arabian Business Magazine Most Influential Arabs 2010
- Arabian Business Magazine Most Influential Arabs 2011
- Foreign Policy Magazine Most Influential Arab Bloggers 2011
- Forbes Most Influential Arabs on Twitter 2011
- Egyptians Against Corruption's Best Anti-Corruption Website 2005

www.ingramcontent.com/pod-product-compliance
Lightning Source LLC
Chambersburg PA
CBHW050520290526
45786CB00007B/2628